MW00861711

# The 7 Habits of Highly Effective People ...in 30 minutes

THE EXPERT GUIDE TO **STEPHEN R. COVEY'S**

# The 7 Habits of Highly Effective People

## ...in 30 minutes

THE 30 MINUTE EXPERT SERIES

GARAMOND PRESS

Copyright © 2013 by Garamond Press. Garamond Press is an imprint of Callisto Media, Inc.

---

**A NOTE TO THE READER: You should purchase and read the book that has been reviewed. This book is meant to accompany a reading of the reviewed book and is neither intended nor offered as a substitute for the reviewed book.**

**This review is unofficial and unauthorized. This book is not authorized, approved, licensed, or endorsed by Stephen R. Covey or Free Press.**

---

Garamond Press and the Garamond Press logo are trademarks of Callisto Media, Inc. and may not be used without written permission. All other trademarks are the property of their respective owners. Unless explicitly stated otherwise, Garamond Press is not associated with any individual, organization, or product mentioned in this book.

No part of this publication may be reproduced, stored in a retrieval system, or transmitted in any form or by any means, except as permitted in accordance with the 1976 United States Copyright Act, without the prior written permission of the publisher. Requests to the Publisher for permission should be sent to permissions@callistomedia.com.

For general information on our other products and services or to obtain technical support, please contact our Customer Care Department at info@callistomedia.com.

The Publisher makes no representations or warranties with respect to the accuracy or completeness of the contents of this work and specifically disclaims all warranties, including, without limitation, warranties of fitness for a particular purpose. No warranty may be created or extended by sales or promotional materials.

The advice and strategies contained herein may not be suitable for every situation. This work is sold with the understanding that the Publisher is not engaged in rendering medical, legal, or other professional advice or services. If professional assistance is required, the services of a competent professional should be sought. The Publisher shall not be liable for damages arising herefrom.

The fact that an individual, organization, or website is referred to in this work in a citation and/or as a potential source of further information does not mean that the Publisher endorses the information the individual, organization, or website may provide or recommendations they/it may make. Further, readers should be aware that websites listed in this work may have changed or disappeared between when this work was written and when it is read.

ISBN: 978-1-62315-149-2 Print | 978-1-62315-150-8 eBook

# Contents

# At a Glance

This book is an extended review of Stephen R. Covey's *The 7 Habits of Highly Effective People*, in which the author notes and describes the effects of a sociocultural shift from what he calls the *Character Ethic* to the values and behavior associated with what he calls the *Personality Ethic*. A common denominator of the Personality Ethic, Covey says, is the habit of blaming external circumstances and other people for personal problems. But Covey sees the development of seven key habits—starting with the habit of taking personal responsibility for personal reactions to life events—as having the power to reverse society's shift to the Personality Ethic, restore the Character Ethic to personal and business interactions, and create the conditions for people's lives to become more meaningful and fulfilling.

The review begins with a four-part section that includes background information about the book and the author, a summary of readers' responses to the book—the good and the not so good, from professional reviewers as well as from bloggers and other interested readers—and a synopsis of *The 7 Habits of Highly Effective People*. That section is followed by a detailed discussion of the book's key concepts. Finally, the main points of this review are briefly restated, in a way that may well inspire you to get your own copy of Stephen Covey's book and see for yourself why *The 7 Habits of Highly Effective People* is such a favorite with readers. Also included are a list of key terms used in *The 7 Habits of Highly Effective People* and recommendations for further reading about what it takes, in terms of character traits and personal qualities, to be successful in business and in every other area of life.

# Understanding
# *The 7 Habits of Highly Effective People*

## ABOUT THE BOOK

First published in 1989, *The 7 Habits of Highly Effective People* has become one of the most popular nonfiction books of all time, as more than two decades of steady sales demonstrate. The idea for the book grew out of Stephen Covey's PhD research. His dissertation topic was American success literature since 1776, for which he conducted a survey of two centuries' worth of nonfiction books and other writings on popular psychology, self-help, and self-improvement.

He discovered that for the first century and a half, this literature urged the development and nurturing of Character Ethic–based qualities like honesty, integrity, and humility, but in the mid-1920s it came to focus much less on character development than on the development of personality traits associated with manipulating others and applying quick-fix solutions to serious, deeply rooted problems. Covey sensed that this change in the literature represented a larger ethical shift. That insight was confirmed when he started noticing the great number of people in contemporary society who seemed emotionally and spiritually adrift, with no clear inner direction.

What brought this home to him, literally, was his perception that one of his children, who was struggling in school and in sports, was not measuring up to his and his wife's standards. After much reflection, Covey realized that his agitation over his son's perceived shortcomings had less to do with the boy's growth and development than with his own concern about how others might be judging him as a parent. Covey and his wife then sought to understand their son by listening deeply to him and seeing him for the person he was, not the one they thought he should be. Their son gradually grew more confident and became successful on his own terms.

Covey drew on his academic research, other work he was doing in the area of perception, and his personal experience with his son to write *The 7 Habits of Highly Effective People*. His goal in writing the book, he says, was to bring about a paradigm shift that would move the reader toward gaining true power and fulfillment in life by taking responsibility for developing and nurturing the personal traits of the Character Ethic.

## ABOUT THE AUTHOR

Stephen Covey was born in Salt Lake City, Utah, in 1932. He was brought up on an egg farm by parents who were devout Mormons, and he continued to follow their faith throughout his life.

Covey was a promising athlete in his youth, but a degenerative disease cut that potential short. He entered the University of Utah at sixteen. After earning a bachelor's degree in business administration, he spent two years in England as a Mormon missionary.

When he returned to the United States, he enrolled at Harvard Business School and earned a master's degree in business administration. After a second mission, this one to Ireland, Covey went back to Utah and earned a doctorate in education and organizational behavior at Brigham Young University, where he also began to teach classes centered on his self-help ideas.

In 1983, Covey founded the Covey Leadership Center, a training and consulting business that later merged with the time-management company Franklin Quest and became FranklinCovey. After *The 7 Habits of Highly Effective People* was published and became a best seller, FranklinCovey became a consulting firm for more than two-thirds of the Fortune 500 companies.

The book's success brought Covey worldwide fame and recognition. In 1994, Covey conferred with President Bill Clinton, and afterward, Clinton said that if people took Covey's counsel, American productivity would soar. In 1996, Covey was named one of *Time* magazine's twenty-five most influential people, and *Forbes* magazine called *The 7 Habits of Highly Effective People* one of the best management books ever published.

In April 2012, at the age of seventy-nine, Stephen Covey lost control of his bicycle on a downhill grade, and he died three months later from complications related to the accident. Covey and his wife Sandra lived in Provo, Utah. They had nine children and fifty-two grandchildren.

# CRITICAL RECEPTION

## *The Upside*

Any book that has sold as many millions of copies as *The 7 Habits of Highly Effective People* is by definition a major influence. In fact, both *Time* and *Forbes* have called it one of the most influential business books of all time.

The book "has solid advice for improving your life," according to the reviewer for HCM Publishing's Bainvestor website, which reviews books on business. The reviewer says further that even though the book makes points that may seem self-evident, there are times when "we might all need to be reminded of the obvious." Similarly, the reviewer for the Mind Tools website says that learning the skills taught in *The 7 Habits of Highly Effective People* can "help you tackle your work and life challenges with new confidence" and that developing Covey's seven habits will "have a lasting effect on your personal effectiveness."

Marc Smith, writing for the *Think Big* blog, says that the book, "if used correctly," can help people "replace old patterns of self-defeating behavior," base relationships on trust instead, and choose patterns of accomplishment and happiness.

Tom Butler-Bowdon, whose website is dedicated to "the literature of possibility," reviews the 1989 edition of the book, noting its crossover appeal to self-help and leadership/management readerships and describing it as a "compelling read." The timing of the book's original publication, he says, was another factor in its success, and in that of the FranklinCovey consulting empire, because by the end of the 1980s, "people were ready for a different prescription for getting what they really wanted out of life."

## The Downside

"Is one of the most popular self-help books ever all it's cracked up to be?" That's the question posed by Duncan Kinney, writing for the online magazine *Unlimited*. Kinney reports trying three times to get through the book and finally taking advantage of a long car trip to listen to the audio version, only to fail again. "There are certain aspects of Covey's arguments that work," Kinney acknowledges, but even the good parts have "a lot of stuff mixed in that is boring and pedantic."

And Stephen Gandel's brief review in *Time*, also of the 1989 edition, doesn't really criticize the book, but Gandel's praise for it is so lukewarm that the review reads almost like a slam. Gandel finds scarce information in the book about either business or management, even though *The 7 Habits of Highly Effective People* is considered a classic in both fields. Instead, he says that what Stephen Covey has written is "a tour de force on confidence building packaged into seven easily digestible maxims" that "overlap and aren't all that revelatory." Nevertheless, he concedes, that hasn't kept the book from continuing to be popular.

# SYNOPSIS

*The 7 Habits of Highly Effective People* is about character development, including the development of such qualities as honesty, integrity, humility, and responsibility. As Stephen Covey points out, qualities cannot be acquired overnight but must be practiced every day until they become deeply ingrained. These four qualities, as well as others, are embodied in the following habits, each of which is discussed in a separate chapter of the book.

Habit 1, *being proactive*, means taking responsibility for your life. Many people believe that their lives have been determined by the conditions around them, by childhood circumstances and events, or by other external forces beyond their control. But Covey says that everyone has free will, imagination, and the ability to choose a response to whatever occurs. If one's response is based on timeless principles, he says, and not on emotionality and impulsivity, then it becomes possible to take control of the situation and the environment.

Habit 2, *beginning with the end in mind*, means visualizing and otherwise vividly imagining a successful outcome before taking on any new endeavor. Visualizing a goal creates a map, Covey says—a guide that shows not only how to reach the goal but also what to focus on along the way. Covey notes that it's also helpful to create a personal mission statement as an aid to staying focused on the things that truly matter in life.

Habit 3, *putting first things first*, means doing what matters most. This habit depends on the priorities we learn to set as a result of developing Habit 2. When we have developed Habit 3, we are willing to do whatever we have to do in order to honor those priorities, even if that means setting aside an impulsive desire to do something more pleasant or exciting. This is the way we develop integrity, Covey says.

Habit 4, *thinking win/win*, means seeking to cooperate rather than compete. In a zero-sum game, Covey explains, there is a winner and there is a loser with nothing in between, and the same dynamic marks a dysfunctional relationship—one person has to lose so the other can win. For Covey, however, the best result is a win for both parties, whether in a personal relationship or a business deal. This is another way to talk about following the Golden Rule.

Habit 5, *seeking first to understand, then to be understood,* means making listening more important than speaking. Far too often, Covey says, people simply react to others' comments, complaints, and opinions, rather than formulate a response that is based on listening to what is being said. But Covey says that real trust and empathy can be developed when people listen to and truly hear one another's words as well the meaning behind them.

Habit 6, *synergizing,* means looking for opportunities to blend your own and others' creativity and energy. As Covey explains, when the creative energies of two or more people are combined, the result adds up to something greater than just the sum of its parts. Cooperation and empathy, he says, set the stage for the kind of open interaction that leads to creative synergy.

Habit 7, *sharpening the saw,* means maintaining the conditions in which your practice of the other six habits can flourish. In order to sustain the kind of personal success that Covey describes as the outcome of developing Habits 1 through 6, there must be regular self-renewal at the physical, mental, spiritual, and emotional levels, he says. Covey calls this multilevel practice of self-renewal "sharpening the saw," using the analogy of a man who has been working hard for many hours to saw down a tree without success, because he has not stopped to sharpen his dull blade so he can accomplish the task.

# Key Concepts of
# *The 7 Habits of Highly Effective People*

According to Stephen Covey, true personal effectiveness requires the development of three kinds of behavior: **choosing the Character Ethic over the Personality Ethic, looking inward before reaching out,** and **renewing all four dimensions of being** (that is, the physical, mental, spiritual, and emotional dimensions).

## I. CHOOSING THE CHARACTER ETHIC OVER THE PERSONALITY ETHIC

Stephen Covey believes that much of today's value system in modern American culture is organized around what he calls the Personality Ethic, the success model that relies on superficial attitudes and behavior, various kinds of manipulation, and positive thinking. Covey sees some good in certain aspects of that model, but he believes that what is far more crucial today is a return to the Character Ethic as well as to widespread social acceptance of and support for demonstrating the values of integrity, humility, courage, and simplicity, and for following the Golden Rule.

For Covey, one of the primary differences between Character Ethic–based change and Personality Ethic–based change is that a transformation of character cannot be accomplished overnight, whereas most Personality

Ethic–based change is the product of quick-fix solutions to deeply rooted problems, which can be held below the surface for a time but are always ready to reemerge. Successful eradication of obstacles to long-term success and fulfillment, Covey says, depends on developing habits that are based on the Character Ethic. Covey believes that these habits, if practiced daily, can slowly but surely improve the way we see and respond to problems, soften hard edges in our relationships, create opportunities for us to launch new projects and enterprises, help us check off the most important items (not just the most urgent ones) on our to-do lists, and show us the path to the genuine and lasting satisfaction of a life well lived.

Accomplishing this kind of change requires us to bring about what Covey calls a *paradigm shift*. A paradigm, he explains, is a model or map for viewing the world—that is, for filtering and conditioning our perceptions, which in turn create the template for how we will react to situations and circumstances. For example, if we believe that our problems are created by external forces—by people and circumstances outside ourselves—then we construct and act from a paradigm of victimhood, which then creates perceptions of personal failure accompanied by defensiveness, despair, anger, and greatly diminished options for success. But if we form the habit of believing that we have the power to choose our responses to external forces, then many new possibilities open up for us, since we no longer experience ourselves as victims of forces we can't control. With this change, we move away from a paradigm of victimhood and adopt a paradigm of personal power derived from unchanging, fundamentally truthful, Character Ethic-based principles. Covey identifies them as fairness, integrity, honesty, human dignity, service, quality/excellence, potential, patience, nurturance, and encouragement. These principles are not the same as values, he says, because even criminals can share values (unfairness, dishonesty, selfishness, and so on) that violate fundamental principles. To make this idea clear, Covey uses an analogy—principles are the territory, and values are the maps. People who value the correct principles gain knowledge of the way things truly are, he says. For Covey, these Character Ethic–based principles are natural, immutable laws—when they're honored, the consequences are positive, and when they're ignored, the consequences are negative, but natural laws always carry consequences.

Covey acknowledges that these Character Ethic–based principles are not easy to adopt and cannot be developed quickly. To flourish they need time, effort, and nurturance, he says, which is why they're so often bypassed in favor of the Personality Ethic and its flashier, trendier, temporary solutions to long-standing problems.

To move from the Personality Ethic to the Character Ethic, Covey says, requires the careful cultivation of his Seven Habits, which should be developed in order. Covey characterizes progress in developing these habits as points along what he calls the *maturity continuum*, which marks the movement from dependence (often involving the paradigm of being a victim) to independence (involving a paradigm of taking responsibility for our experience) and ultimately to interdependence (involving the paradigm of combining our own and others' gifts and efforts to create something greater than the sum of its parts).

## *Examples from* The 7 Habits of Highly Effective People

* Stephen Covey tells the story of how he experienced an instant paradigm shift while riding on the subway in New York. A man boarded the train with two children, who became extremely unruly and disturbed the other passengers while the man sat back with his eyes closed and appeared to ignore their behavior. When Covey politely asked him to rein the two youngsters in, the man opened his eyes, seemed to become aware of the situation for the first time, and explained that he and the children were on their way back from the hospital where their mother had just died. Covey's perception of the situation changed at once, dramatically, and he quickly moved from being annoyed to feeling sad and wondering how he could help.

- As another illustration of a paradigm shift, Covey relates an apocryphal anecdote about a U.S. Navy captain conducting training maneuvers on a battleship in foggy weather. As night fell, a strong light appeared in the distance, and the captain ordered his signalman to tell the oncoming ship that it needed to change course. A message came back that the captain needed to change his own course. This exchange of messages was repeated, and finally the frustrated captain radioed, "I am a battleship. Change course 20 degrees." The return message was "I am a lighthouse." The captain changed course. (For more background on this well-worn urban legend, see "The Obstinate Lighthouse" at Snopes.com.)

## *Applying the Concept*

- **The Character Ethic in marriage.** Marriage is prime terrain for getting stuck emotionally—specifically, for developing the habit of blaming your spouse for problems. Instead of looking at all your reasons for being angry or frustrated with your spouse, take a look at your own behavior. Are there things you're saying or doing that might be contributing to the situation? If you're willing to examine and take responsibility for your own behavior, the marriage you save could be your own.

- **The Character Ethic in parenting.** Do you really know your children? Or instead—even with the best of intentions and aided and abetted by your natural concern for your children's welfare—are you critical of their behavior, their tastes in music or fashion, their friends, and so forth, because you unconsciously see them as extensions of yourself? Ask yourself this question the next time your child does something to embarrass you or make you feel like a bad parent: Is it possible that you would have a different reaction if you were less concerned about your image and more curious about how your child sees the world and what your child deeply values?

- **The Character Ethic in the workplace.** What would your workplace be like if your manager stopped worrying about whether you and other employees are sufficiently dedicated? What would it feel like for you to go to work and never have to complain again about your unsympathetic manager or about unappreciative customers? How might your workplace change if the higher-ups started asking themselves how they could be more responsive to their employees' needs and desires? How might your workplace change if you put yourself in their shoes and thought about what you could do to allay their concern about productivity, or if you put yourself in your customers' place and thought about how you could improve their experience?

## II. LOOKING INWARD BEFORE REACHING OUT

Stephen Covey says that there are certain actions that need to be taken in a particular order before the process of living by Character Ethic–based principles can begin. Each of these steps must be internalized through daily practice until it becomes a habit, which Covey defines as the intersection of knowledge, skills, and desire, all three of which he says must be present before a habit can be formed.

The first three of the Seven Habits, which involve looking inward, take us from a starting point of dependence, or relying on other people and external situations for happiness, to independence, or becoming responsible for our own happiness. Habit 1 is *being proactive*, or developing and acting on the belief that we can choose our behavior instead of allowing our behavior to be dictated by our circumstances. Habit 2 is *beginning with the end in mind*, which includes having a vivid and clear vision of the desired outcome before embarking on any important endeavor. Habit 3 is *putting first things first*, which for Covey means making sure that after we've attended to anything that is both important and urgent (such as a fire in the kitchen), we turn next to things that are important but *not* urgent (such as meditating or organizing our files) and forgo things that are urgent but unimportant (such as showing up at an appointed time to participate in an unnecessary meeting) or not urgent and not important (such as mindlessly watching TV).

The next three of the Seven Habits, which involve reaching out to others, take us from independence to interdependence, the basis for collaborations whose results would be impossible for any one person to create alone. Habit 4 is *thinking win/win,* or looking for ways to satisfy everyone involved in a negotiation and make everyone successful. (Obviously, win/win solutions have no place in warfare or a game like chess, but they are often possible in business and other areas of life. And if a win/win solution isn't possible in a particular situation, Covey says it's probably best just to walk away.) Habit 5 is *seeking first to understand, then to be understood,* which means really listening to what other people are saying instead of using their words as a launching pad for our own remarks. Habit 6 is *synergizing,* which depends on recognizing the skills and talents of others so we can join them in creating something that adds up to more than just the sum of its parts.

## *Examples from* The 7 Habits of Highly Effective People

- Stephen Covey makes a clear distinction between language that is proactive and language that is reactive, and he lists many examples of reactive language—statements like *That's just the way it is* and *I really wish we didn't have to* . . . and *There just isn't time* and *It makes me so furious* and *If only* . . . . The basic statement underlying all these others, he says, is *I am not in control of my responses to situations*—or, more succinctly, *I am not responsible.* In this way, Covey calls explicit attention to how people use reactive language to absolve themselves of responsibility for their behavior, their choices, and the quality of their lives.

- Covey makes a distinction between what is urgent and what is important. Some urgent situations are also important; these are usually emergencies of some kind. Other urgent situations are not important at all, no matter how much excitement or pleasure they may involve, or how much pressure we feel to behave as if such situations deserve our immediate attention. But some of the most important things we can do—planning, spending time with friends, exercising, performing various kinds of maintenance, getting a mammogram, learning another language—are not urgent, and so we tell ourselves we'll get around to them. And this, Covey says, is why we often let the most important things in life slide, wasting our precious time on things that are urgent but unimportant, or on things that are neither urgent nor important. Covey says the key to effective time management, and therefore to real results in life, is to keep our focus on the things that are most important to us, especially when those things don't demand our immediate attention and action.

## Applying the Concept

- **What really matters?** Imagine that yesterday was the last day of your life, and write your obituary. Then read it. What does it say about who you were and what you did with your time on the planet? Are there things you wish you could change? Are there things you wish you had done differently? Does reading about your life bring to mind any missed opportunities? Write down your answers to these questions, and use your answers to make a list of things you still have time to change and goals you can still accomplish.

- **See your future today.** Now that you've examined your life and come face-to-face with what really matters to you, choose one change or goal to focus on. Take a few minutes to imagine yourself as you will be when you have made this change or accomplished this goal. How do you look in this situation? How do you dress? How old are you? Are there new people in your life? Does your life include people you already know, but in new roles? How do you feel when you wake up every morning? Continue imagining your new situation, bringing in as many of your senses as possible so you can make it as real to your body as it is to your mind.

- **Let's make a deal.** If you have an important negotiation coming up, whether at work or with a friend or family member, now is the time to practice looking inward before reaching out. If you've been feeling that you're at the mercy of the situation to be discussed, search your mind and emotions for signs of the victim paradigm, and remember that even though you can't control every aspect of the situation, you can choose how you will respond to it. Take some time to imagine the outcome you want. If necessary, find the time to visualize that outcome by letting go of less important activities or commitments. Now begin reaching out— mentally at first, by thinking about outcomes that might be of benefit not just for you but also for the other party, and then interpersonally, maybe by practicing your listening skills with someone you trust. Continue reaching out, if only in the privacy of your thoughts, by bringing to mind some strengths and talents that you appreciate in your negotiation partner, qualities that complement your own and would create synergy in any negotiated solution that the two of you reach.

## III. RENEWING ALL FOUR DIMENSIONS OF BEING

Habit 7, which Stephen Covey says penetrates all the others, is caring for the four dimensions of ourselves: physical, mental, spiritual, and emotional. Covey believes that if we don't regularly renew these four aspects of ourselves—and what he means by "regularly" is "every day"—we won't be able to sustain our practice of the other six habits. Covey calls Habit 7 *sharpening the saw*, a reference to the need for steady maintenance of our most important tools. It can be a challenge to renew these aspects of ourselves, Covey says, because doing so involves daily activities and tasks that, while crucially important, are not urgent.

In the physical dimension, Covey cites healthful food, lots of rest, and regular exercise as important aspects of a daily routine—and, not incidentally, as crucial factors in enhancing self-esteem and self-confidence. In the mental dimension, he urges using discretion when watching television, and he encourages reading good books, writing letters instead of using e-mail, and perhaps keeping a journal. In the very private spiritual dimension, Covey suggests daily meditation, prayer, communing with nature, or otherwise strengthening what he calls the "leadership center of our lives," which we depend on for strength, courage, and wisdom. And in the emotional dimension, Covey says renewal is about genuinely connecting with others every day by seeking mutually successful outcomes, listening deeply, and finding opportunities for synergy—in other words, by practicing Habits 4, 5, and 6. He cautions that neglecting any one of the four dimensions will have negative repercussions for the others.

## *Examples from* The 7 Habits of Highly Effective People

- In order to build new muscle tissue, Covey says, it may be necessary to strain the existing muscle tissue to the breaking point. When breakage occurs, the muscles rebuild themselves and are even stronger than before. Covey says the same principle can work with our emotional and mental "muscles." But he cautions that just as with our physical muscles, we shouldn't overdo emotional or mental things to the point where we stop enjoying the experience.

- Spiritual renewal can mean different things to different people. Covey recounts an anecdote titled "The Turn of the Tide" from *A Touch of Wonder*, a book of inspirational essays by Arthur Gordon. In that essay,

Gordon writes about a time when he lacked motivation and energy and thought that his life had no value. Things got so bad that he made an appointment to see his doctor. The doctor got out his prescription pad, wrote out four prescriptions, put them in sealed envelopes, and sent Gordon off with instructions to go to the beach and open one prescription every four hours. When Gordon opened the first prescription, it simply told him to listen. The second prescription told him to reach back, and Gordon relived many important moments of his life. The third prescription told him to examine his motives, and Gordon discovered that he didn't like them at all because they were about personal success, not about service to others. The fourth and final prescription told him to write his worries in the sand, and Gordon did, knowing that the tide would soon wash them away.

## Applying the Concept

- **Death and taxes.** They're both as certain as ever, but at least when it comes to filing your tax return, you know when your time is up. If you've fallen into the habit of waiting until April 14 to start organizing your records and receipts, give yourself the gift of everything you need—account books, file folders, tax-preparation software, and the like—to put your financial house in order. Then take a few minutes every day to record your daily income and expenses. Paying this kind of steady attention to your finances won't feel or be as urgent as scrambling to meet the tax deadline, but it's important work that will free your time for things you'd rather be doing, such as walking your dog or running or playing tennis or riding your bike—and possibly getting an extension on that other deadline.

- **Stormy weather.** There are times when the metaphor of the economic climate seems like more than a figure of speech, and that's true for many people today whose economic "weather" has been severe for several years. In these conditions, it can be difficult if not impossible to believe there's any possibility of choosing how to react to the continuing economic downturn—and forget about visualizing a more prosperous future. If that's your situation, remember to take good care of yourself every day. Going for a stroll in a beautiful place won't put money in your pocket, but it just might lift your mood enough to change your outlook and bring you the kind of inner calm that produces mental clarity—and maybe even the presence of mind to spot a business opportunity that will chase the clouds away.

- **Screening interview.** If someone asked you how much time you spend every week in front of a screen, would you even know how to answer? Make sure you can. This week, keep a diary of your screen time. How much time do you spend watching television? How much time do you spend surfing the Web? How often do you actively choose to spend your time this way? How often is watching TV or surfing the Web something you do reflexively? How much do you really enjoy your time in front of the TV or the computer, or the time you spend with your iPad and other devices? By the end of the week, you should be able to say how much screen time you have in your life. More than that, you should be able to say whether you feel it's important for you to spend your time this way, and if you do, why it's important. And if it's not important, you'll know that, too, and you can give some thought to how you really want to spend your time.

## Key Takeaways

- Stephen Covey believes that a paradigm shift occurred in American culture shortly after World War I and that the Personality Ethic replaced the Character Ethic in popular conceptions of what it means to be successful in life. Covey urges a return to the Character Ethic and its time-tested principles, which he says will serve as a solid foundation for anyone as he or she faces life's challenges.

- According to Stephen Covey, if we start by looking inward (being proactive in our lives, envisioning successful outcomes, doing what really needs to be done), we establish the basic habits we need for reaching out (seeking mutually beneficial outcomes, listening deeply, seeking synergy). Together, the acts of looking inward and then reaching out encompass the first six of the Seven Habits, which form the core of Covey's book.

- In order to practice the first six habits in a real and consistent way, Stephen Covey says, we need to develop Habit 7: daily renewal of the physical, mental, spiritual, and emotional dimensions of our lives. Whenever one of the four is out of balance, that imbalance adversely affects the other dimensions, Covey says, but when we practice Habit 7, we sustain our ability to practice Habits 1 through 6.

# A Final Word

*The 7 Habits of Highly Effective People* is one of the most popular and best-selling management and self-help books of all time. Since its original 1989 edition, the book has been inspiring  people to take a long, hard look at themselves and decide what really matters in life.

In the years between the book's first publication and his death in 2012, Covey managed to parlay his book's success into a virtual *7 Habits* franchise, a multimillion-dollar enterprise that offers tools for consulting and time management as well as other products and programs using the concepts outlined in the original and later editions. The book's popularity may stem from its core premise: that too much emphasis has been placed on personality and not enough on character. Other self-help and success-oriented books focus on positive thinking, social manipulation, and quick fixes for problems, but Covey thought that many of our problems are too deeply rooted to be solved with quick fixes. What is needed instead, he believed, is a paradigm shift that can restore the lost emphasis on character—on such qualities as honesty, integrity, humility, and fidelity, which cannot be developed overnight but must be practiced every day until they become habits.

This review has offered you a glimpse of Stephen R. Covey's *The 7 Habits of Highly Effective People.* The best way to continue learning about the character traits most important to true success, and therefore to what Covey sees as deep happiness and fulfillment, is to buy a copy of the book, absorb its lessons, and see how well Covey's approach and conclusions match with your own perceptions and experience.

# Key Terms

**abundance mentality**   a view of the world that acknowledges the existence of plentiful resources. Stephen Covey says that adopting this perception and turning away from a focus on what is missing can have a powerfully positive effect on personal responses to specific situations and to life in general.

**beginning with the end in mind**   the second of the **Seven Habits**. At the beginning of a project, situation, or any kind of endeavor, Covey says, visualization of the intended goal can chart a clear path to the desired outcome.

**center**   for Stephen Covey, the primary place from which someone sees the world. The center, he says, is also the place where principles are evaluated and truths are intuited.

**Character Ethic**   what Stephen Covey sees as the **paradigm** of success, as defined by a life of deep meaning and value. For Covey, the Character Ethic is embodied in personal humility, integrity, courage, and patience, among other qualities, as well as in the principle of following the Golden Rule.

**Circle of Concern**   the name Stephen Covey gives to a diagram representing phenomena and events that a person cares about but has little or no power to affect or control. A person's Circle of Concern might encompass the federal deficit or the problems and behavior of celebrities, for example. Covey suggests that this diagram be used in conjunction with the **Circle of Influence** to distinguish what merely feeds emotional responses from what can actually be controlled. He says that focusing attention on the Circle of Concern leads to becoming disempowered and feeling controlled by events, other people, and similar external forces.

**Circle of Influence**  the name Stephen Covey gives to a diagram representing phenomena and events that a person both cares about and has significant ability to affect and control. A person's Circle of Influence might encompass his or her perceptions, diet and exercise habits, and willingness to be a deep listener, for example. Covey suggests that this diagram be used in conjunction with the **Circle of Concern** to distinguish what can actually be controlled from what merely feeds emotional responses. He says that focusing attention on the Circle of Influence leads to becoming self-empowered and gaining more control over those things that can be controlled.

**Emotional Bank Account**  Stephen Covey's metaphor for the amount of trust in a relationship. Actions involving such qualities as honesty, integrity, humility, and deep listening all constitute "deposits" to the Emotional Bank Account, whereas such actions as lying, cheating, and reacting without thinking constitute "withdrawals" from the account. The goal is to have a high balance of trust.

**empathic communication**  the embodiment of the fifth of the **Seven Habits**. Stephen Covey says that most of us listen to others only halfheartedly because we're already formulating a response while others are still speaking. This type of behavior leaves no room for us to really hear either what was said or the emotions behind the words. Covey says we can let others know that we've heard them and that we're sincerely trying to understand them, by deeply listening to them, paraphrasing what they've just said, and including an interpretation of the feelings behind their words.

**habits**  for Stephen Covey, behavior reflecting the intersection of three elements: knowledge, skill, and desire. Covey uses the term *knowledge* to mean both the action that will be performed and the reasons for performing it, the term *skill* to mean the way in which the action should be performed, and the term *desire* to mean a personal wish to perform the action. In order for any action to become a habit, Covey says, all three elements must be present.

**the inside-out approach**   the name Stephen Covey gives to the practice of seeing many personal problems as rooted in personal responses to external forces rather than in those forces themselves. Covey says that the adoption of this perceptual framework represents a major **paradigm shift** from the **Personality Ethic** to the **Character Ethic**.

**maturity continuum**   the sequence of growth stages that Stephen Covey says people pass through as they adopt the **Seven Habits**. Covey characterizes progress along the continuum as movement from dependence (reliance on others) to independence (self-reliance) and finally to interdependence (engagement with others to make connections and to create).

**paradigm**   a metaphorical model or map for perceiving, interpreting, and understanding the world. Stephen Covey says that the **Character Ethic** and the **Personality Ethic** are both examples of paradigms.

**paradigm shift**   the outcome of questioning, evaluating, and changing the views and assumptions that constitute a **paradigm**. Stephen Covey lists a number of examples of paradigm shifts, but perhaps the one most relevant to the **Seven Habits** is the return he envisions to the **Character Ethic** after many years of the **Personality Ethic**'s dominant influence.

**Personality Ethic**   what Stephen Covey sees as the **paradigm** for the quick fixes often promoted by self-help and success-oriented books. Such literature, he says, tends to be organized around values involving social manipulation, positive thinking, public image, and techniques borrowed from the field of public relations.

**P/PC balance**   Stephen Covey's formula for sustainability, where *P* stands for *production of desired results* and *PC* stands for *production capability*, or the ability to continue producing the desired results. Covey introduces this formula with the classic tale of the greedy, impatient farmer who killed the goose that laid golden eggs because he wanted to gather all her eggs at once instead of waiting for her to produce them day by day. He also offers the example of his own lawn mower, which worked for two seasons but became useless because he failed to keep it in working order. In the same way, he says, there must be balance in business relationships: if the focus is exclusively on production, then the means of production will wear out, but if there is too much attention to the means, then there will be far less production.

**private victory**   successful development of the first three of the **Seven Habits**. Stephen Covey says that internalization of each of these three **habits** is a private victory because all three have to do with the individual.

**public victory**   successful development of the fourth, fifth, and sixth of the **Seven Habits**. Stephen Covey says that internalization of each of these three **habits** is a public victory because all three require interaction with others.

**Seven Habits**   the particular set of **habits** that Stephen Covey associates with the **paradigm shift** represented by restoration of the **Character Ethic**. Covey defines these habits as (1) being proactive, (2) **beginning with the end in mind**, (3) putting first things first, (4) thinking win/win, (5) seeking first to understand, then to be understood, (6) synergizing, and (7) doing what he calls "sharpening the saw," that is, doing whatever is necessary to ensure that the values and behavior of the Character Ethic will be sustainable over the long term.

**synergy**   a phenomenon that becomes possible when two or more people join their talents, skills, and perceptions. When synergy occurs, Stephen Covey says, something is created that no single individual could have achieved alone.

**time management matrix**   the four-quadrant diagram that Stephen Covey uses to illustrate his approach to setting priorities. In Quadrant I of the matrix are crises, pressing problems, and deadlines—things that are both important and urgent. Quadrant II is for activities like planning, prevention, maintenance, recreation, relationship building—things that are just as important as those in Quadrant I but that are not urgent. Quadrant III is where interruptions are found—many types of phone calls, e-mail messages, meetings, and other things that are often confused with those in Quadrant I but that are actually not important, even though they may seem urgent because an in-the-moment response is encouraged or expected. In Quadrant IV are busywork, mindless TV watching, and other wastes of time—things that are neither important nor urgent. Covey says that most people spend too much time in Quadrants I, III, and IV, and not enough time in Quadrant II.

# Recommended Reading

In addition to the revised edition of Stephen R. Covey's ***The 7 Habits of Highly Effective People*** (Free Press, 2004), the following books are recommended for anyone who wants to learn more about the personal and characterological foundations of success in business and personal life.

### David Allen, *Getting Things Done: The Art of Stress-Free Productivity* (Viking, 2001)

According to David Allen, a coach and management consultant, productivity is directly proportional to the ability to relax. The first section of Allen's book outlines his five-part process for stress-free productivity. The second section offers the nuts and bolts of the process, and the third section shares insights into its advantages.

### Kenneth Blanchard and Spencer Johnson, *The One Minute Manager* (William Morrow, 1982)

This business classic tells the tale of a young man who searches for great management skills and finds three—setting goals, offering praise, and issuing reprimands, and always in just one minute.

### Dale Carnegie, *How to Win Friends and Influence People*, reissue edition (Simon & Schuster, 2009)

*How to Win Friends and Influence People,* which first appeared in 1936 during the Great Depression, is one of the best-known books ever published in the fields of self-help and business success, a perennial favorite still being published in hardcover format. This classic text has taught generations of readers how to stop being manipulated, make themselves heard and appreciated, and find success by expressing their ideas.

**Stephen M. R. Covey with Stephen R. Covey and Rebecca R. Merrill, *The Speed of Trust: The One Thing That Changes Everything* (Free Press, 2006)**
In this book, the son of Stephen R. Covey, working with a collaborator, examines the need for trust and illustrates his points with examples from the lives of thirteen trusted leaders whose attributes include transparency and respect, as well as other qualities.

**Stephen R. Covey, *The 8th Habit: From Effectiveness to Greatness* (Free Press, 2004)**
This book, a follow-up to *The 7 Habits of Highly Effective People,* was written for readers in what Stephen R. Covey calls "the Knowledge Worker Age." The "habit" in the title is that of finding a unique personal voice and inspiring others to find theirs.

**Napoleon Hill, *Think and Grow Rich* (Napoleon Hill Foundation, 2012)**
First published in 1937, this book has been a best seller ever since. It is the product of twenty years of research that the author undertook, using a large group of successful people. He then developed a series of "laws for success" and condensed them to the thirteen steps he outlines in this self-help classic.

**Jim Loehr and Tony Schwartz, *The Power of Full Engagement: Managing Energy, Not Time, Is the Key to High Performance and Personal Renewal* (Free Press, 2003)**
Managing time is important, these two authors say, but to be most effective and fulfilled, people usually have a greater need to learn how to manage their energy. The authors have both been involved in training athletes, and so they approach the subject of energy management from the standpoint of personal experience.

**John C. Maxwell,** *The 21 Irrefutable Laws of Leadership: Follow Them and People Will Follow You,* **10th revised and updated edition (Thomas Nelson, 2007)**

First published in 1998, this book shares insights from the author's life as a pastor and business leader. The fundamental keys to effective leadership, he believes, include learning how to be influential, read people, intuit trends, give away power, and create forward motion.

# Bibliography

**Tom Butler-Bowdon, *"The 7 Habits of Highly Effective People* (1989), Stephen R. Covey"**

*Tom Butler-Bowdon*, undated (accessed April 5, 2013)

http://www.butler-bowdon.com/sevenhabits

**Stephen Gandel, *"The 7 Habits of Highly Effective People* (1989), by Stephen R. Covey"**

*Time*, August 9, 2011 (accessed April 17, 2013)

http://www.time.com/time/specials/packages/
article/0,28804,2086680_2086683_2087685,00.html

**Arthur Gordon, *A Touch of Wonder: A Book to Help People Stay in Love with Life***

Old Tappan, NJ: F. H. Revell Co., 1974

**Duncan Kinney, "Book Review— *7 Habits of Highly Effective People"***

*Unlimited*, June 1, 2010 (accessed April 17, 2013)

http://www.unlimitedmagazine.com/2010/06/book-review-
7-habits-of-effective-people

**"The Obstinate Lighthouse"**

Snopes.com, last modified April 2, 2012 (accessed April 18, 2013)

http://www.snopes.com/military/lighthouse.asp

**"*The Seven Habits of Highly Effective People*: Learning to Manage and Live Life in an Effective and People-Focused Way"**
Mind Tools, undated (accessed April 17, 2013)
http://www.mindtools.com/pages/article/newLDR_79.htm

**"*The Seven Habits of Highly Effective People: Restoring the Character Ethic*, by Stephen R. Covey"**
Bainvestor.com, undated (accessed April 17, 2013)
http://www.bainvestor.com/Seven-habits-effectiveness-Covey.html

**Marc Smith, "Book Review: *The 7 Habits of Highly Effective People*, by Stephen Covey"**
*Think Big* (blog), September 14, 2011 (accessed April 5, 2013)
http://thinkbigproject.blogspot.com/2011/09/book-review-7-habits-of-highly.html

CPSIA information can be obtained at www.ICGtesting.com
Printed in the USA
LVOW06s1924180813

348431LV00001B/188/P